HOW TO TURN YOUR BLING HOBBY INTO A LUCRATIVE BLING BRAND

by **YATARA REED**

Bling Like A Boss

©2020 Orange Sleeve, LLC

ALL RIGHTS RESERVED

As this workbook is interactive, you are welcome to print a copy of this document for personal use. Outside of personal use, no part of this text may be reproduced, distributed, or transmitted in any form or by any means, including photocopying, recording or other electronic or mechanical methods, except as permitted under Section 107 or 108 of the 1976 United States Copyright Act, without the prior written permission of 'The Bling Academy / Orange Sleeve, LLC'.

LIMITATION OF LIABILITY/DISCLAIMER OF WARRANTY:
Although a wealth of knowledge from years of trial and error has been compressed into workbook form, we can make no assurance as to any particular financial outcome based on the use of this guide. No warranty may be created or extended by sales representatives, promoters, or written sales materials.

You agree that The Bling Academy / Orange Sleeve, LLC is not responsible for your earnings, the success or failure of your personal or business decisions, the increase or decrease of your finances or income level, or any other result of any kind that you may have as a result of information presented to you through our website or informational products offered.

The advice and strategies contained herein may not be suitable for your situation. You should consult with a professional where appropriate. Neither the publisher nor author shall be liable for any loss of profit or any other commercial damages, including but not limited to special, incidental, consequential, or other damages.

You are solely responsible for your results. Any testimonials used are of actual clients and results they personally achieved, or they are comments from individuals who can speak to my character and/or the quality of my work. They are not intended to represent or guarantee that current or future clients will achieve the same or similar results; rather, these testimonials represent what is possible for illustrative purposes only.

For questions and permission requests, please feel free to contact to the publisher at admin@theblingacademy.com.

contents

Segment I - Dearly Beloved

Welcome..7

Laying the foundation.......................................10

Segment II - Taking Care of Business

Get your Concept! 17
    What is your business idea?

Get your Compass!...23
    What is the plan for your business?

Get your Capital! 27
    How will you finance your business?

Get your Corp! 33
    How will your business be structured legally?

Get your Certification! 37
    Have you registered with your State and the Federal Government?

Get your Coverage! 41
    How is your business protected?

contents
continued

Get your Character! 47
How is your business branded?

Get your Carts! 53
Who are your suppliers?

Get your Crew! 61
Who is on your team?

Get your Community! 67
Who is following your brand?

Get your Customers! 73
How will you attract new buyers?

Get your Coins! 77
How are you processing payments?

Segment III - Work Smarter not Harder

contents
continued

Website Checklist	83
Password Log	84
Stationary/Packaging Checklist	85
Product Pricing Formula	87
Order Form	88
Income/Expense Tracker	89
Rhinestones Size Chart	91
Placement Patterns	92
Tu - TOE - rial	93
20 Projects (to launch your bling business)	95
30 Day Display Challenge	96
Project Planner	98
Additional Resources	99

Yatara Talise

WELCOME

If you are reading this that means you've made a conscious decision to officially start your bling business OR you've decided to take your bling business to the next level... either way, The Bling Academy's 'Bling Like A Boss' is just the tool you need.

There are two ways to gain knowledge... (1) from personal experiences and (2) from the experiences of others. Learning from the experiences of others is waaaaaay less expensive, less time consuming and less painful than figuring things out on your own.

'Bling Like A Boss' was created out of a passion and desire to help you earn additional income doing what you love and to assist you in your desire to transition from blinging as a simple relaxing hobby, or side hustle, to producing items for your own organized, recognizable and lucrative brand.

That being said, thank you for your purchase and for allowing me to share information, strategies, techniques and tools that I have acquired and personally implemented over the past 10 years to establish my bling repertoire, increase my production rate and alleviate financial pressures.

In this workbook you'll find general topics that you can customize to build your own bling brand. Please keep in mind, as you are laying your foundation, the information provided is only intended to serve as a launching pad to get you started. Additional research will be necessary to meet your needs and to discover specific business requirements of your local area.

Also included are Q & A's and fillable sections in the various stages of launching your brand that will help you to elaborate, structure and prioritize your thoughts. I understand how overwhelming building a brand can be. Many times I wished I had a step-by-step guide or someone who was GENUINELY interested in laying out a path for me to follow. I couldn't find exactly what I needed all in one place, so I decided to compile lessons learned and create this workbook for anyone who may need a little help getting to the next level. I may not know your name but I definitely had you in mind!!

If at any time you have general questions, want to share your journey or need words of encouragement, feel free to reach out to me via email at admin@theblingacademy.com or send a private message via facebook or instagram to '@theblingacademy'. I've included images of a few of my creations throughout the workbook for your inspiration.

It's my desire to help you bling officially!
It's my desire to help you bling efficiently!
It's my desire to help you **'Bling Like A Boss'**!!

Let's GOOOOOO!

Segment I

Dearly beloved...

we are gathered here today to join together your dreams, your goals, your desires and your reality.

Vow everyday to remain optimistic, consistent and persistent throughout your journey. As the years pass, you will celebrate on this day,

_____
(mm/dd/yyyy)

the anniversary of the day you committed to make your **DREAM a REALITY!!**

Laying the Foundation
See It Before You Can See It

As with any new or modified endeavor there will be many ups, downs and turns on the road to what you define as success. Success is a very personal journey and although the road is the same, everyone's trip will be different depending on their destination.

Every lane is not for everyone and neither is every exit. Speed varies based on prior experience or how quickly you learn a technique. Your journey is personal... not competitive. Never compare your beginning to someone else's current situation. There's a process that must be followed. Trust it! Trust the journey.

To reach YOUR destination you must see where you want to end up even before you begin the journey. What does success look like to you? Again... success is personal. How will you handle course corrections that need to be made along the way?

Before we go on, let's take a moment to answer a few questions that will help you as you move forward.

Why do you want to create / expand this business? (What drives you? / What fuels your passion?)

This answer will remind you to keep going even when you don't "feel" like it.

_____
_____
_____
_____
_____

What will you have to sacrifice in order to build your business?

This answer is a reality check! Some things may have to be set aside as you focus.

_____
_____
_____
_____
_____

How will your background or experience help you to make this business a success?

This answer establishes your credibility.

_____
_____
_____
_____

What is the name of your business?
This answer will differentiate you from your competitors.
_____
_____
_____
_____
_____

Who is your customer?
The answer will assist you in building your client base as well as when creating the branding package for your business.
_____
_____
_____
_____
_____

What type of products are your customers looking to purchase?
The answer will help you as you build your line of products.
_____
_____
_____
_____
_____

Who are your mentors? (If you don't have any, begin following people who are successful in your field.)
The answer will give you inspiration and watching their productivity will spark your creativity.

_____
_____
_____
_____

What contributed to their successes?
This answer will teach you valuable "DOs" without the trial and errors attached.

_____
_____
_____
_____

What contributed to their failures?
This answer will teach you valuable "DONTs" without the expense of first hand knowledge.

_____
_____
_____
_____

What are their price ranges?

This answer will help you as you look to price similar products competitively.

_____
_____
_____
_____
_____
_____

How do they market their work?

This answer will provide inspiration and a success model.

_____
_____
_____
_____
_____
_____

How can you modify your product based on what you've learned?

This answer will help your productivity.

_____
_____
_____
_____
_____
_____

As you continue on to segment II you will elaborate on the answers that you've provided here. Your preliminary responses will be very useful as you begin to dive deeper into developing your brand.

consistency births success

THE BLING ACADEMY

Segment II

TAKING CARE OF BUSINESS

Get Your Concept!

Get Your Concept!
What is your business idea?

Since you've made it this far you obviously don't need to come up with a business idea, you have that covered. Bling is your business! However, you don't want to be so broad in what you offer that you spread yourself too thin. What is your specialty?

Start with a few items and master those. Work on increasing your production rate. As you become more efficient in your production feel free to add on. If you try to take on everything at once there's a great possibility that you'll become overwhelmed.

At one point I was working on shoes, tumblers, keychains, dominoes, bridal bouquets, car accessories, conference props, phone cases, headphones, centerpieces, stuff, stuff and some more stuff LOL!! Its great to be able to offer so many things, but I've found that its better to find your niche, master it and charge for your expertise.

Why make 10 items at $15 each when you can create 1 custom item and charge $150? Find out what works best for you then WORK IT!!

Now... let's take a look back at the mentors you listed in the foundation segment. Do they have a specific product line or do they offer any item that is "blingable"? (LOL... that our new word!!)

If they offer multiple products, how many? Are they fast production items such as keychains or more intricately designed products such as phone cases or bling shoes?

What are they doing that you can do just as well or even better? What are their current rates? What is their turn around time to deliver a finished product? How can you improve upon what's already on the market? How is your product different?

Please note.... this is **<u>NOT</u>** research for the purpose of copying the work of others, however, it's important to understand your competitors (or future collaborators) and the market that you share.

On the following page list the inspirational companies and makers that you've identified and any significant notes to remember about them.

Digital Mentors

Company	Social Media Account
1.	
2.	
3.	
4.	
5.	
6.	
7.	
8.	
9.	
10.	

NOTES _____

_____
_____
_____
_____
_____
_____

Digital Mentors

NOTES

TRUST THE PROCESS

Get Your Compass!
What is the plan for your business?

YOU MUST PLAN IN ORDER TO SUCCEED!! If you fail to plan… you most certainly plan to fail. Your business will not succeed just because you want it to. Everything will not be perfect as a result of a wish. There will be many days and nights of hard work ahead but they will come and go much easier if you have a written plan in place.

Your business plan is your roadmap to success; success that is, as YOU have defined it. It should state your purpose, state your goals, identify your client, indicate how much money is needed to start and where the initial finances will come from. You can also include projected monthly expenses and income.

Let's get a bird's eye view of your bling business.

How would you describe your business?

_____
_____
_____
_____
_____
_____

How do you define success as it relates to your business?

What is your primary goal as a company?

How is your business unique?

Why would a potential customer choose you over a competitor?

List some the items that you'd like to offer your clients.

_____
_____
_____
_____
_____

Will you offer customized items? List a few of your ideas below.

_____
_____
_____
_____
_____

What is the approximate time frame needed to produce each item?

_____
_____
_____
_____
_____

3
Get Your Capital!

Get Your Capital!
How will you finance your business?

Blinging as a hobby can be expensive especially if you're like me and want every stone you see in every size and color available. When starting a business it is very necessary to make non-emotional financial decisions. Be sure to spend the minimum amount required and make sure that it's only on the things that are essential for the business to grow and be a success.

There are many questions that need to be answered in order to create a sound financial plan.

Do you have money saved to start your business?
[ ]   Yes.   How will it be allocated to meet your business needs?
[ ]   No.   What steps can you take to acquire funds?

_____
_____
_____
_____
_____
_____

How much money is needed to begin?

_____
_____
_____
_____

Will you need to borrow money to start your business?

_____
_____
_____
_____

Do you need investors? If yes, how will you find them?

_____
_____
_____
_____

How much is needed to cover all expenses over a 3 month time span? 6 months? 9 months? 12 months?

_____
_____
_____
_____
_____

What items and quantities are necessary to start your business?

_____
_____
_____
_____
_____

Which products show a profit and which ones are sold at a loss? (if you are currently selling products)

_____
_____
_____
_____
_____

Use the chart on the following page to help get an idea of the finances you'll need to jumpstart your business. Some line items can be left blank to be filled in at a later date. If more space is needed, feel free to copy the page to complete the task.

Start-Up Capital Worksheet

Start-up Item needed	Have or need?	Notes	Cost
Business Licenses			
Incorporation Expenses			
Initial Branding Design			
Equipment/Supplies			
Insurance			
Inventory			
		Total Startup Expenses:	

CREATE YOUR OWN OPPORTUNITIES

Get Your Corp!

4

Get Your Corp!
How will your business be structured legally?

Before registering your business, you must decide what type of entity it will be. The structure of your business will determine tax practices as well as what you could be personally liable for in the event something unexpected happens.

Research the various types of corporations and note the pros and cons for each.

Sole Proprietorship

PROS:	CONS:

Partnership

PROS:	CONS:

Limited Liability Corporation (LLC)

PROS:
_____
_____
_____
_____

CONS:
_____
_____
_____
_____

Corporations

PROS:
_____
_____
_____
_____

CONS:
_____
_____
_____
_____

Based on your research and needs, which type of entity is the best option for you? Why?

NOTES _____
_____
_____
_____
_____
_____

NOTES

5 Get Your Certification!

Get Your Certification!
Have you registered with your State / Federal Government?

In order to be recognized as an official business by the government you must register your company. Corporations will need to have an "articles of incorporation" document. It should include your business name, purpose, corporate structure, stock details and any other information about your company you'd like on file.

Research the specific requirements for your city and state as well as any associated fees.

After you've registered with your state, you may need to get an Employer Identification Number (EIN) from the IRS. Whether or not you need an EIN will depend on how you structure your business. Make sure you have researched and chosen the structure best suited for you. If you in fact do need an EIN, you can register online and download your letter for free.

Be sure to check with your city and state to find out if you need a seller's permit that authorizes your business to collect sales tax from your customers.

📝 NOTES

NEVER give up on YOURSELF

Get Your Coverage!
How is your business protected?

Imagine working on a project and making a wrong turn only to see your rhinestones flying in all directions. Imagine spilling a massive amount of glitter that will take daaaaaays to thoroughly clean up. Imagine being overcome with the feeling of helplessness. Now.... imagine those feelings of horror magnified 10 times over caused by something completely out of your hands.

You may not think insurance is necessary when your just starting out on such a small scale but it absolutely is. Take a moment to answer the follow questions before you decide to skip this section.

 Have you or will you invest a considerable amount of money into your business?

 If there were a flood, fire or natural disaster, would it hurt your business?

 Do you or will you travel with your supplies or products to vendor events or shows?

 Can someone be injured or their property be damaged by your product?

If you have answered yes to any of these questions, then it is extremely important that you get insurance coverage for your business. Always expect the unexpected. You could possibly experience an accident, theft, property damage or worse case scenario… a customer could file a lawsuit. You want to be protected no matter the case…. and no matter the size of your business.

If your business will be home-based, you can possibly add an endorsement to cover your equipment and supplies. Contact your local insurance agent for the best policy that suits your needs. DON'T WAIT!!

If you currently have supplies, do an inventory check to come up with the value of your tools, equipment and product. This will help your agent put a quote together for you.

Start-up Inventory Value

Item	Description	Qty	Value

Start-up Inventory Value

Item	Description	Qty	Value

NOTES

7
Get Your
Character!

Get Your Character!
How is your business branded?

What character traits describe your business? What should come to mind when customers hear your business name? What should a potential client see when reading a business card or flyer for your product? What feeling is attached to your product? What are the meanings of your color choices?

There are many components to creating your company's character or branding your company. After deciding your name and understanding your mission, an entire package should be created. The right branding will attract new customers. Brand recognition, and quality of service, will draw repeat clients. Your brand, in summary, is a promise to your clients regarding what they will experience with your company.

Whether you work with a graphic designer or choose to do research and create your brand on your own, you'll need to have an outline for your design plan.

To inspire you, I've included a few elements that were presented in the brand package created for The Bling Academy.

Answer the following questions to help as you map out your plan to create a branding package for your business.

What is Your Mission?

Your mission statement should include your company's goals and explain what, how and why your company does what it does for its customers.

_____
_____
_____
_____
_____

What is Your Tagline?

Your tagline is a memorable catch phrase or slogan that helps your customer identify your brand.

_____
_____
_____
_____
_____

#015B68   #79C4CA   #D7B411

Who is your target demographic?

This will help when determining how to cater the branding to be attractive to your target audience.

_____

_____

_____

_____

_____

What is your color palate?

Colors have meaning and evoke a specific emotional response. Choose colors that line up with what you'd like to communicate to your customers.

_____

_____

_____

_____

_____

What are you trying to achieve with your logo?

Your logo design is basically a symbol that represents you and distinguishes your products from other companies.

_____
_____
_____
_____
_____

What fonts best fit your brand?

Your fonts are specific designs of letters used **consistently** when representing your brand. Select 2-3 to use in headers, sub-headers and body text.

_____
_____
_____
_____
_____

How will your brand be displayed?

Each media format uses different dimensions. (facebook, website etc.) Knowing how and where your brand will be displayed will help when laying out multiple versions of a particular image for your brand.

_____
_____
_____
_____
_____

What is the long term goal for your brand?

Brands take time to build. Long term goals for your brand will help you establish what you'd like to see in the future and visualize beyond where you are at the moment.

_____
_____
_____
_____
_____
_____
_____

Get Your Carts!
Who are your suppliers?

The best way to stay ahead of your bling orders is having an updated cart list. You can also think of your cart as an inventory list that shows what you've purchased, when you purchased it, the quantity, the cost and from whom. (This list may be kick-started from the inventory list created for insurance purposes.)

Creating your cart list can be tedious and a bit overwhelming if you currently have a mountain of rhinestones and other craft supplies. Do not get discouraged. Take a day or two or seven (LOL) to review what you have on hand and log it. If you're just getting started, log the items and organize them as soon as you take them out of the bag (or box). It's much easier to list items as you move forward rather than trying to recap your purchases later.

Having this list can help you make cost saving decisions by comparing suppliers' pricing. Wholesale options for things you use more frequently than others should be considered as well.

As you create your cart list, take this time to organize your supplies so they are visible and easily attainable. Knowing what you have (or don't have) before you need it will help decrease possible expedited shipping fees.

Your cart list can not only include everything that you use to produce your product but I'd suggest using it to keep a running tab on your promotional products as well.

Imagine reaching for a business card or flyer only to realize you need to place an order to get more. Again, staying ahead of your needs saves money in the long run especially as it relates to the additional costs of expedited shipping.

Use the cart list on the following pages to help you get organized and stay ahead of items that need to be reordered.

Side note:
It may also be beneficial for you to list any items you use to store your products as well. Over the years I've tried many different types of containers. I've come to recognize that I work best using clear storage containers for items I use most often and more opaque containers (matching the office decor of course) for items needed less frequently.

The image below is how I store my rhinestones and track inventory for future orders.

RHINESTONES

Vendor	Color	Size	Quality	Quantity	$/per	Last Ordered
Sample The Crystal House	Lt. Siam	16ss	Resin	5,000	$5/1000	5/2020

RHINESTONES

Vendor	Color	Size	Quality	Quantity	$/per	Last Ordered

Add to Cart

MISC. SUPPLIES

Vendors	Item	Quantity	$/per	Last Ordered
Sample DIY 4 YOU	Sorting Trays	10	$10/10	3/2020

MISC. SUPPLIES

Vendors	Item	Quantity	$/per	Last Ordered

THE REST is just as important as THE GRIND!

Get Your Crew!
Who is on your team?

As you began to grow and get more bling orders you will need help. Your team may not necessarily make the items you sell but they can assist in processing orders, preparing shipments, social media marketing and interaction, inventory, vendor events etc. Whomever you choose to add to your team, make sure they have a clear understanding of your purpose, your market, your client and your product.

Team members, in the beginning, don't necessarily have to be paid staff. They could simply be individuals who believe in your dream and have a desire to help you make it come true. Team members could include your spouse, children, best friend, brother, sister etc... anyone who is willing to commit to keep pushing you forward so that you, one day, physically see everything that you've imagined.

Take a moment to visualize your business as a well-oiled, perfectly running machine. What departments are needed and how does each area function? Identify each role that will be needed for your business to run successfully. What is the responsibility of each role? Even if you are not yet prepared to fullfill a particular position, still include it in your list so that you will have a written description prepared when the time comes.

Who Do I Need? _____
(title / position)

What do I need them to do?_____
(job description / responsibility)
_____
_____
_____
_____
_____

Who Do I Need? _____
(title / position)

What do I need them to do?_____
(job description / responsibility)
_____
_____
_____
_____
_____

Who Do I Need? _____
(title / position)

What do I need them to do?_____
(job description / responsibility)
_____
_____
_____
_____
_____

Who Do I Need? _____
(title / position)

What do I need them to do?_____
(job description / responsibility)

_____
_____
_____
_____
_____

Who Do I Need? _____
(title / position)

What do I need them to do?_____
(job description / responsibility)

_____
_____
_____
_____
_____

Who Do I Need? _____
(title / position)

What do I need them to do?_____
(job description / responsibility)

_____
_____
_____
_____
_____

Who Do I Need? _____
(title / position)

What do I need them to do?_____
(job description / responsibility)
_____
_____
_____
_____

Who Do I Need? _____
(title / position)

What do I need them to do?_____
(job description / responsibility)
_____
_____
_____
_____

Who Do I Need? _____
(title / position)

What do I need them to do?_____
(job description / responsibility)
_____
_____
_____
_____

Do it For Your FUTURE Self!

THE BLING ACADEMY

Get Your Community!
Who is following your brand?

How many times have you visited a new restaurant based on a friend's recommendation? How many movies have you seen because someone talked about how good it was? How many products have you tried based on rave reviews?

They say that word of mouth is the best advertisement (and its free). Social media can be used to rapidly get the word out about you, your business and your product. It all begins with 1 post... 1 like... 1 share... 1 comment... and not necessarily from a customer but from an admirer of your work. GIVE THEM SOMETHING TO TALK ABOUT!

Think of social media as an online mall and each follower as a potential shopper OR a potential advertiser for your business. Your timeline is the window to your business. Be sure to display your products and your personality. Yes, your personality!

Social media requires that you are just that… Social! Take time to interact in the comment sections of your various platforms. Brands are important but people follow and connect with people. As an introvert, I understand how scary that can be… trust me, I struggle with posting, commenting and pretty much everything involved with social media other than scrolling and admiring the work of the creators I follow.

I'm definitely learning that you must consistently post images and videos of your work in order to see an increase in views and engagement. Again, socialize with those who comment on your timeline. You'd be amazed how 10 minutes of responding to comments and regular post engagements will increase brand recognition and awareness.

There are many who have social media expertise that you can follow or even hire to give you more insight in this area. On the following page I'll share the outline that is really helping me. Now remember... social media IS NOT MY THANG...LOL! I'm a blinger. The exampled outline is what I created after a few online searches and Pinterest saves. Full disclosure: I'm still a work in progress in this area!

DIRECTIONS:
Each box represents 1 day within a 1 month time frame. Enter content that you'd like to post on your business' social media pages each day. It could be a video / photo of various products, a share of something that inspires you or an encouraging quote. Fill each box as you see fit. If you're overwhelmed, start with 3 days per week, work your way up to five then seven.

Remember to use consistant hashtags and to respond to comments. Also, create goals for each week... how many post likes... page likes... new followers, etc. There are many content templates online if you need ideas. The only right way is the way that works for you and your business.

Monthly Posting Schedule

In each box below note what you'd like to post on your social media accounts.
It could be a photo / video of your work, a personal photo / video or an encouraging message.
Remember to respond to any questions or comments.

	Day 1	Day 2	Day 3	Day 4	Day 5	Day 6	Day 7
Week 1							
Week 2							
Week 3							
Week 4							

GOALS

Week 1: _____
_____
_____
_____
_____
_____

Week 2: _____
_____
_____
_____
_____
_____

Week 3: _____
_____
_____
_____
_____
_____

Week 4: _____
_____
_____
_____
_____
_____

DUPLICATE AS NEEDED

Use the space below to list hashtags unique to your bling brand. When creating or listing your tags remember the following...

1. Keep it **Simple** and easy to remember.
2. Keep it **Consistent** on all of your platforms.
3. Keep it **Current** with what's popular.
4. Keep it **Minimal** using only a few tags per post.
5. Keep it **Relevant** to your services.

NEVER FORGET YOUR WHY!

THE BLING® ACADEMY

Get Your Customer!
How will you attract new buyers?

There are hundreds of people (if not thousands) who want, need and are looking for your services but they don't know you exist... **YET**. Exposure is crucial to the success of your company; but once potential customers have been referred to you or have come across your hashtags in a random search, how are you reeling them in? What's the point of exposure if you can not convert them to a paying customer?

It is imperative that you have an active website to ensure that you are not missing out on additional exposure, inquiries and sales. Your website is the hub that will help past, present and future customers find specific answers as it relates to your products, services, business structure, policies etc. History and credibility can be established by including testimonials and customer reviews.

Including an online shop will allow you to give very detailed descriptions of your products, display pictures from various angles and essentially make money while you sleep. The sky is the limit!

Again... Your customers are searching for you! You have what they want and need. Make it easy for them to hear about you. Make it easy for them to find you. Make it easy for them to buy from you! Make it easy for them to COME BACK TO YOU!!

Here are a few simple ideas to help attract new buyers.
- ☑ Keep your platforms current
- ☑ Participate in vendor events
- ☑ Ask for referrals
- ☑ Offer freebies
- ☑ Follow up with inquiries
- ☑ Offer 'new customer' discounts
- ☑ Create buy-one-get-one offers
- ☑ Offer your expertise
- ☑ Build partnerships with other brands

List additional strategies that you'd like to incorporate into your marketing plan to get new clients and increase your customer base.

Get Your Coins!
How are you processing payments?

Your business is not your hobby. Hobbies are for fun and relaxation. It is a wonderful thing to be able to grow a business doing what you love to do, but you have to treat it as a BUSINESS… a for-profit business who's goal is to MAKE MONEY! Favors are ok! Bartering is ok! Freebies are ok... **HOWEVER**... you have to make the transition from constantly 'doing a favor for someone' to 'processing a paid order' for a customer. Know your worth... charge for your expertise... allow for profit and add tax!

Ok... now that we've made that clear, what system(s) do you have in place to process payments? Cash is great but "cash-only" limits you to physical in-person transactions. By selecting a payment processor and connecting it to your website you will be able to broaden your customer base and receive payments from all around the world. You'll also have the ability to collect customer information for future sales.

Research payment processing options that are available to you through your selected hosting platform as well as those that can be connected externally. Decide which best fits your business needs.

Payment Processing Options

	PROS:	CONS:
Website's merchant account options:		
Paypal:		
Cashapp:		
Square:		
Zelle:		

Payment Processing Options

	PROS:	CONS:
Other:	_____ _____ _____ _____ _____	_____ _____ _____ _____ _____
Other:	_____ _____ _____ _____ _____	_____ _____ _____ _____ _____
Other:	_____ _____ _____ _____ _____	_____ _____ _____ _____ _____
Other:	_____ _____ _____ _____ _____	_____ _____ _____ _____ _____
Other:	_____ _____ _____ _____ _____	_____ _____ _____ _____ _____

Segment III
TOOL BOX

Work Smarter not Harder

Website Checklist

[_] Have you secured your domain name?

[_] Have you selected a website host?

[_] Do you have a home page?

[_] Have you included a "call to action"?

[_] Do you have an About Page?

[_] Do you have a Contact Page?

[_] Are your social media accounts connected?

[_] Is your branding consistent?

[_] Did you check for spelling errors?

[_] Is your site user friendly?

[_] Are all links working correctly?

[_] Does your website display correctly on all devices?

[_] Have you included your terms of service?

[_] Do you have product photos and vivid descriptions?

[_] Are you able to process payments?

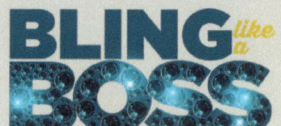

Passwords

Website: _____

- Username: _____
- Password: _____
- Email Linked: _____
- Security Question: _____
- Security Answer: _____
- Notes: _____

Website: _____

- Username: _____
- Password: _____
- Email Linked: _____
- Security Question: _____
- Security Answer: _____
- Notes: _____

Website: _____

- Username: _____
- Password: _____
- Email Linked: _____
- Security Question: _____
- Security Answer: _____
- Notes: _____

Website: _____

- Username: _____
- Password: _____
- Email Linked: _____
- Security Question: _____
- Security Answer: _____
- Notes: _____

Website: _____

- Username: _____
- Password: _____
- Email Linked: _____
- Security Question: _____
- Security Answer: _____
- Notes: _____

Website: _____

- Username: _____
- Password: _____
- Email Linked: _____
- Security Question: _____
- Security Answer: _____
- Notes: _____

Website: _____

- Username: _____
- Password: _____
- Email Linked: _____
- Security Question: _____
- Security Answer: _____
- Notes: _____

Website: _____

- Username: _____
- Password: _____
- Email Linked: _____
- Security Question: _____
- Security Answer: _____
- Notes: _____

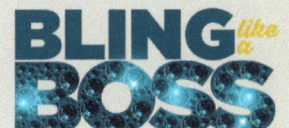 

Stationary / Packaging Checklist

- [_] Order Forms
- [_] Business Cards
- [_] Thank You Cards
- [_] Bubble Wrap
- [_] Stickers
- [_] Boxes
- [_] _____
- [_] _____
- [_] _____
- [_] _____
- [_] _____
- [_] _____
- [_] _____
- [_] _____

- [_] Invoices
- [_] Promo Flyers
- [_] Packing Slips
- [_] Tissue Paper
- [_] Bags
- [_] Shipping Labels
- [_] _____
- [_] _____
- [_] _____
- [_] _____
- [_] _____
- [_] _____
- [_] _____
- [_] _____

Sample PRODUCT PRICING FORMULA

Product Name: _____

A. Supplies
List all physical materials needed to create your product (rhinestones, glue, cabochons etc.)

1 _____ $ _____
2 _____ $ _____
3 _____ $ _____
4 _____ $ _____
5 _____ $ _____

Supply Total:

$ _____

B. Overhead
List miscellaneous items such as utilities, travel, merchant fees, branding, packaging, etc. needed to create your product.

1 _____ $ _____
2 _____ $ _____
3 _____ $ _____
4 _____ $ _____
5 _____ $ _____

Overhead Total:

$ _____

OR Add 10-20% of your supply total.

C. Labor
Pay yourself!! Include yourself or the assigned staff member who created the product.

$ _____ X _____
    Hourly Rate   Hours

Labor Total:

$ _____

TOTAL COST   (A+B+C): $ _____

D. Wholesale Pricing
This is your rate to charge for bulk orders.

$ _____ x 2
    Total Cost

Wholesale Price: $ _____

E. Retail Pricing
This is your rate to charge for individual orders.

$ _____ x 2
    Wholesale Price

Retail Price: $ _____

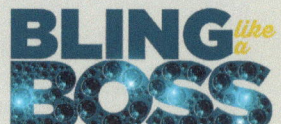

Sample ORDER FORM

Your Name / Logo

Date: _____
Order #: _____
[ ] New   [ ] Return

Name: _____
Shipping: _____
Address: _____
_____

Phone: (____)_____   Email: _____

Shipping Information
Date Shipped: _____
Method: _____
Tracking #: _____
Expected Arrival: _____
Actual Arrival: _____

Order Details

Item #	Description	Qty	Unit Price	Total

Notes: _____
_____
_____

Date Paid: _____   Payment Method: _____

Sub-total: _____
S+H: _____
Tax: _____
Discount: _____
Total: _____

Sample Income / Expense tracker

Date	Description	Amt	Income ($)	Expense ($)

DREAMERS WHO ONLY DREAM WILL ALWAYS ONLY DREAM!

DREAM ABOUT IT THEN DO IT!

RHINESTONE SIZE CHART

RHINESTONE SIZE	DIAMETER(~)
3 ss	1.3 - 1.4 mm
4 ss	1.5 - 1.7 mm
5 ss	1.7 - 1.9 mm
6 ss	1.9 - 2.1 mm
8 ss	2.3 - 2.5 mm
10 ss	2.7 - 2.9 mm
12 ss	3.1 - 3.3 mm
16 ss	3.9 - 4.1 mm
20 ss	4.6 - 4.8 mm
30 ss	6.4 - 6.6 mm
34 ss	7.1 - 7.3 mm
40 ss	8.4 - 8.7 mm

PLACEMENT *Patterns*

Linear Placement
Setting with same sized stones centered both horizontally and vertically.

Honeycomb Placement
Setting with same sized stones centered diagonally or staggered on each row.

Scattered Placement
Setting with multiple stone sizes placed as spacing allows.

Circular Placement
Setting with same sized stones in a circular pattern.

*Extra spacing has been left in diagrams for visual clarity.
When creating your products decide the spacing that best fits your style.

tu - toe - rial

1.
Place your rhinestones in a sorting tray.

2.
Work in small areas and put a thin layer of glue on the toe of your shoe. You can place directly from the tube or use a syringe.

3.
Use the pick-up tool of your choice to set each stone in the glue.

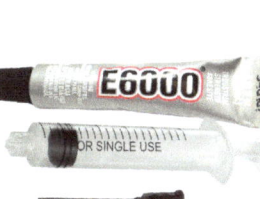

4.
Place stones using the suggested pattern guide. Row count will vary depending on stone size.

- Row 1
- Row 2
- Row 3
- Row 4
- Row 5
- Row 6
- Row 7

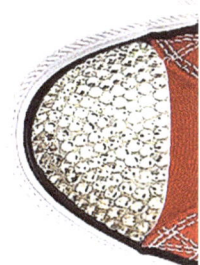

Don't be limited by boundaries that others have placed on themselves.

THE BLING® ACADEMY

20 PROJECTS
TO LAUNCH YOUR BLING BUSINESS

1. Phone cases
2. Charger blocks
3. Masks
4. Keychains
5. Shoes
6. Mirrors
7. Tumblers
8. Headphones
9. Mugs
10. Wine glasses
11. Badge reels
12. Baby shoes
13. Rollerskates
14. Phone grips
15. Make up brush sets
16. Home decor lettering
17. Picture frames
18. Refrigerator magnets
19. Sports jerseys / hats
20. Sports equipment / balls

Challenge

30 Day Display

Create a list of products to complete over a 30 day period. Take pictures of each item and have a mass sale at the end of the 30 days.

Day 1: _____   Day 16: _____

Day 2: _____   Day 17: _____

Day 3: _____   Day 18: _____

Day 4: _____   Day 19: _____

Day 5: _____   Day 20: _____

Day 6: _____   Day 21: _____

Day 7: _____   Day 22: _____

Day 8: _____   Day 23: _____

Day 9: _____   Day 24: _____

Day 10: _____   Day 25: _____

Day 11: _____   Day 26: _____

Day 12: _____   Day 27: _____

Day 13: _____   Day 28: _____

Day 14: _____   Day 29: _____

Day 15: _____   Day 30: _____

Use the hashtags **#theblingacademy** and **#30daydisplay** in addition to your hashtags so that we can share in your success!!

Don't be disappointed by a no. A no directs you to your yes.

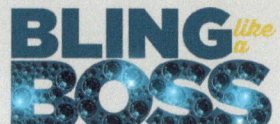

Sample Project Planner

Week: _____

MONDAY

TUESDAY

WEDNESDAY

THURSDAY

FRIDAY

SATURDAY

SUNDAY

todo this week

- [ ] _____
- [ ] _____
- [ ] _____
- [ ] _____
- [ ] _____
- [ ] _____
- [ ] _____
- [ ] _____
- [ ] _____
- [ ] _____
- [ ] _____
- [ ] _____
- [ ] _____
- [ ] _____
- [ ] _____
- [ ] _____
- [ ] _____
- [ ] _____
- [ ] _____
- [ ] _____

notes

_____
_____
_____
_____
_____
_____

Additional Resources

I Talk to Myself:
90 Affirmations for Creative Minds
is a great tool that will help negate the insecurities that sometimes manifest during the creative process. It will assist in fostering positivity, encouragement and confidence as ideas are given life outside of the imagination.

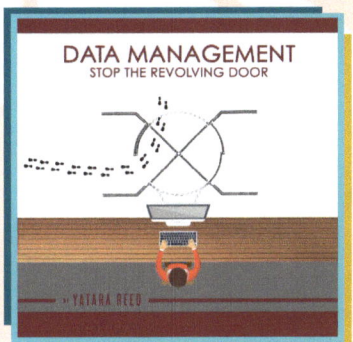

Data Management: Stop the Revolving Door
Discover techniques and strategies to help you maintain your customers, clients and ministry team members by strategically using and maintaining your database.

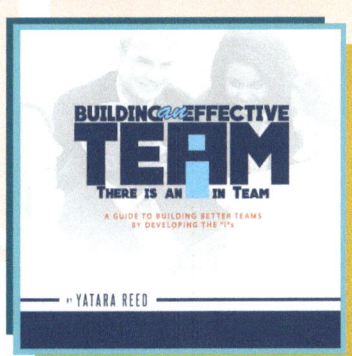

Building an Effective Team:
There is an I in Team
Discover the attributes of an effective leader as well as those of an effective team. Explore principles and a few of the essential characteristics that are necessary to help you build and develop your team.

Attribution:

All pictures of finished 'bling' products shown throughout this publication have been hand crafted by the author.

Branding elements designed by 4thgencreations.com

Chapter icons have been designed using resources from Flaticon.com

BLING like a BOSS

THE BLING ACADEMY

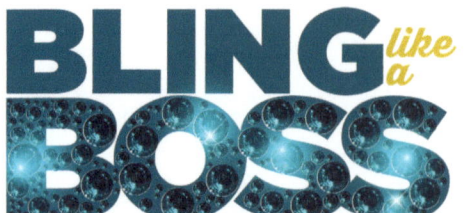

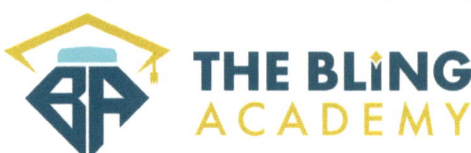

www.theblingacademy.com

admin@theblingacademy.com

313.920.0969

https://www.facebook.com/theblingacademy

https://www.instagram.com/theblingacademy

www.ingramcontent.com/pod-product-compliance
Lightning Source LLC
Chambersburg PA
CBHW041701160426
43191CB00003B/52